Mia Marconi has an Italian father and an Irish mother. She grew up in London and has been a foster carer here for over 20 years. During that time she has welcomed more than 250 children into her home. To protect the identities of people she is writing under a pseudonym.

*Also by Mia Marconi:*

*Learning to Love Amy*
The foster carer who saved
a mother and a daughter
Mia Marconi
HarperTrueLife

*If Only He'd Told Me*
A foster family
pushed to the limits
Mia Marconi
HarperTrueLife

*Little Girl Lost*
The true story of a broken child
Mia Marconi
HarperTrueLife

# A Child
# Called Hope

# A Child Called Hope

The true story of a
foster mother's love

Mia Marconi

with Sally Beck

Certain details in this story, including names, places and dates, have been changed to protect the family's privacy.

HarperTrueLife
An imprint of HarperCollins*Publishers*
77–85 Fulham Palace Road,
Hammersmith, London W6 8JB

www.harpertrue.com
www.harpercollins.co.uk

First published by HarperTrueLife 2014

1 3 5 7 9 10 8 6 4 2

© Mia Marconi and Sally Beck 2014

Mia Marconi and Sally Beck assert the moral
right to be identified as the authors of this work

A catalogue record of this book is
available from the British Library

PB ISBN: 978-0-00-810505-1
EB ISBN: 978-0-00-758442-0

# Chapter One

Dad walked through the door and handed me an orange chopper bike. In the early Seventies, choppers, with their extended front forks and small wheels, were the *only* bike any child wanted, and now I was the first child on my street to get one.

My dark, handsome dad loved to be generous when he could and he knew that the only thing I really wanted was a chopper. So when he handed it over I was so happy I began screaming and shouting and running round our flat in Bermondsey in south-east London. Mum's face was a picture – not of happiness but of fury. She began screaming and shouting at Dad because we didn't have any money and he had just spent what he'd won on the horses on a bike, not the rent. As the row heated up, I waited for them to start throwing pots and pans at each other, but Dad walked out in a huff and we didn't see him for three days.

\*   \*   \*

Dad was born during the Second World War in Italy in a breathtakingly beautiful little village called Altomonte. It was mainly populated then by peasant farmers (living off the land rather than making a living from it) and is in the region of Calabria. Most people know Calabria, which is tucked away in southern Italy in the toe of the boot, because of the 'Ndrangheta – the Calabrian Mafia – who became notorious for smuggling and kidnapping wealthy northerners, hiding them in the mountains and holding them for ransom.

Actually, when they were all dressed up, Dad's family did look quite like mafiosi, with their short, sturdy figures, black clothes and their weather-beaten faces framed by immaculately backcombed or brilliantined hair. But they were honest, simple people, toughened up by hard work. There was a real sense of community where they lived and if someone got sick, the village would rally round and deliver them a little extra food.

Altomonte is such a beautiful, hilly place and the only area in the world that can grow large quantities of bergamot flowers – their essential oil is used in perfumes and Earl Grey tea, and you never forget their musky scent. The plants, with their pale blue flowers, are everywhere, and just like a good strong cuppa they make me feel incredibly calm and peaceful whenever I see them.

In spite of the 'Ndrangheta, Altomonte is also

very spiritual, almost a place of pilgrimage. It sits on a hilltop, dominated by a breathtakingly beautiful fourteenth-century white church, or basilica, which shines out across the hillside like a holy beacon.

Just being in the village can give you goose bumps, which has something to do that church. It's called Santa Maria della Consolazione and it doesn't matter where you are in the village – having a glass of wine in the piazza in the evening or drinking a morning coffee in one of the little cafés close by – you can hear hymns being sung by the nuns and monks, and the gentle sound is carried across the village on the breeze. It's a place where you think, nothing bad can happen here. But something terrible did happen, and it happened to my grandmother.

My family's story begins in a battered old farmhouse in Altomonte where my great-grandmother and great-grandfather raised ten children and one grandchild – my father. Dad was happy in that farmhouse, but his childhood was cut short when he was just eleven, the day he found out the truth about his birth. His story went swiftly from one about a contented country boy who had a future working the land to one of secrets, rejection and survival.

He discovered that his mother, Rita – my grandmother – was ripped from the heart of her family after a scandal that could not be healed.

It's hard to describe how very close Rita was to her brothers and sister, but as the second eldest, she had a special bond with them. They'd grown up in the same farmhouse, in the same small community, in a family that had lived there for generations.

They were extremely poor, but Dad said they always had a dinner on the table, because the land fed them. When the crops failed or they ran out of food, they would go out foraging, picking figs or apples off trees in the surrounding hills, or asking the other farmers if they had any extra. Neighbours obliged when they could, because they knew that when they were struggling, my father's family would happily help them out in return. They had all looked out for each other and shared each other's secrets, but despite that, my grandmother was forced by her family to leave home when she was just twenty-three, and told never to come back. She never, ever got over it, and she lived until she was eighty-three.

My pretty, raven-haired grandmother, Rita Marconi, had committed the worst sin any Catholic girl could commit. Unmarried, she had slept with a man and got pregnant. I don't know about their relationship, whether it was a quick fling in a field or whether they'd been seeing each other for a while, but the story goes that to try to get him to marry her, her eight brothers beat him up. He still would not put a ring on her finger and a single mother in those days brought shame on her family. Overnight, Rita went from being a much-loved daughter to a problem they had to deal with.

# A Child Called Hope

It was 1942, halfway through the Second World War and the Mediterranean surrounding Calabria had already been the scene of a pitched battle between the Italian, British and Australian navies. Life was uncertain, but one thing was sure: there was no way an unmarried mother would be accepted by the religious community, and no way she could live peacefully at home. There were no second chances if you made a slip up like that, and for Rita the consequences were harsh. After her son Benito (my father) was born, she was taken to the convent and forced to have a hysterectomy, which was performed by the nuns, so that there could never be a chance of her slipping up again. Her only sister told me years later that she had kicked and screamed and fought to escape but was overpowered when they sedated her with chloroform. When she was in her forties, she was told by the doctors here that she had been butchered.

As if that wasn't bad enough, she was banished from Altomonte, without her son – her mother brought him up as her own – and sent to live with family friends in the port of Reggio Calabria.

Reggio Calabria is the main town in Calabria, and the main launching point for ferries sailing to Sicily. Although it is in the same province as Altomonte, the two places are 150 miles apart, and in the days when public transport was scarce, none of her siblings would be sneaking away to visit her, so for the first time in her life, Rita knew what it felt like to be alone.

By the time she arrived in Reggio Calabria, the port town was full of soldiers and marines looking for a good time. At the local piazza, where all the young people congregated, she met a British soldier called Harry Burns. He was a man with a reputation who dabbled in the black market, the man you went to if you needed a pair of stockings or a pack of cigarettes. He had made a name for himself and he had money to throw around. Whether or not Rita really fell in love with him I am not certain – maybe she just wanted to escape – but she married him and they moved to a tiny flat in Brixton, south London.

She probably thought she would never see her son Benito again, but by the time he was eleven both Rita's parents had died and none of her siblings could, or would, look after him. Up until then, Benito had thought that his grandparents were his parents. You can only imagine the shock he felt when they broke the news to him that he was illegitimate and that his real mother was living in England. He was not the youngest in the family any more, because his grandmother had had their tenth child and Benito thought he had a younger brother, although really he was his uncle.

As his family turned their backs on him, the pattern of banishment began again; he was now following in his mother's footsteps. He must have been so frightened having to leave everything he had ever known, being sent to a country he had probably only ever heard mentioned a few times, to live with a woman he had never met, even if he had been told she was his mother. You would have thought that Rita would have been delighted to be reunited with him, but she didn't want him with her and didn't hide the fact. Consequently, she was always very cold and distant with him.

According to my mum, she did really love him but had no idea how to show it. I never saw her give him a kiss or a cuddle, and she was never affectionate towards us, her grandchildren. It was confusing, though, because when we all went back to Italy together she would change. In England she always seemed depressed, but in Altomonte she seemed to come alive. Nothing would stop her kissing and cuddling her brothers' and sister's children; she made a proper fuss of them. That must have destroyed my dad. It really upset me, because I could never understand why she would not kiss and cuddle me, her own granddaughter.

If we were at a big family gathering in Italy, and Rita suddenly became sociable and happy, Dad and I would catch each other's eye, and that look said that we both felt really sad. Dad longed for his mother to love him and I longed for my grand-mother to love me, but she never softened, not once in all those years. I still cannot understand why, but there was never the tiniest chink in her armour.

It might have been different if Dad's own father had ever acknowledged him; then at least he would have had one parent to love. He did try to get to know him – when he was twenty-three he felt strong enough to go and find his father. Dad flew to Italy and spoke to his uncles, who knew exactly where to find the man who had refused to marry their sister all those years ago. He still lived in the same village and they saw him often.

Initially, they were not sure it was a good idea when Dad asked, but reluctantly they agreed to introduce him. It took all his courage and strength, but one afternoon he set off with an uncle to meet his father. In a strange coincidence, they met him walking along the street, and Dad could not believe how alike they looked. They were virtually identical, he said, and could have been brothers. Sheepishly, he walked over to him and said in Italian: 'Excuse me, I am your son.' Dad's life could have changed in that minute if his father had given him a great big bear hug, but instead he spat right into his face. That despicable act could not have caused more pain if he had fired both barrels of a shotgun at him at point-blank range.

When Dad told me that story I could not understand the coldness of his father. I simply could not comprehend how someone could harbour so much hatred for their own flesh and blood. It was a savage rejection that I will never unravel, no matter how hard I try.

I made a real effort to accept my nan, Rita. I knew she had loved village life and had been forced to leave it all behind. She had loved her brothers and sister and had been forced to leave them too, so every time she looked at my dad, all she saw was the reason she wasn't living the life she wanted. I always felt like she actually really hated him when he was around her. That was probably worse than the rejection by his father, because he had to deal with her coldness towards him on a daily basis. There was no escape for Dad. Where most of us have our lives shaped by love, Dad's was shaped by constant rejection.

So by the time he met my mum, Rose, he was pretty angry, and it was a recipe for disaster. I think he was looking to be mothered, but Mum couldn't fill in those missing years. Dad was very needy, but so was she; she had her own insecurities.

# Chapter Two

Mum's parents were from Ireland and they ended up in Catford, south-east London. Where they lived was badly bombed during the Blitz, so their home was surrounded by shattered buildings, but they knew they were the lucky ones. They still had a home.

It might have looked ugly, but the children loved clambering over the piles of rubble, looking for little bits of shrapnel. What they were desperate to find was a real bomb – *that* was the prize – but thankfully, they never did.

Mum's father was soft and gentle and genuine, but drink did not agree with him. If he'd spent the night in the pub he could turn violent, and on those occasions my grandmother, like so many women, would be on the receiving end of his frustrations.

Nan became adept at hiding the bruises and honestly gave as good as she got, using a big heavy frying pan to defend herself. Sometimes they could both be seen with black eyes, their hats pulled down over their faces in an effort to disguise their battle scars, but the neighbours knew what was happening. It was happening to some of them too.

Friday night was always dangerous, because the minute Granddad received his pay packet, he would head for his local, The Black Swan, or 'The Mucky Duck' as they nicknamed it. He would stay there, laughing with his pals and drinking brown ale, until he got hungry and wanted his tea. When he opened the front door, Mum would be on red alert. As soon as she detected the tell-tale smell of brown ale on his breath, she knew that it would all kick off and there would be a fight. That was her cue to run upstairs, wake her younger brother Patrick, get him up and walk him round the streets until she thought it was safe to go back home. Sometimes close neighbours (whom they called Auntie and Uncle, although they were not related) would invite them in. As many of them knew the situation, if they saw Mum and Patrick walking round late at night, hand in hand, they would let them sit by the fire until things calmed down. Mum said that there was many a time when she and Patrick fell asleep in someone else's house.

Despite the fact that he drank and became violent, Mum idolised her dad, and he never hit his kids. He wasn't always drunk and he loved my mum and Patrick. She remembers sitting on his knee and feeling the rough stubble on his chin. She also remembers how he would sometimes bring home little bits of shrapnel for their collection and, very occasionally, produce a bag of sweets from deep in his jacket pocket.

My granddad was an ambulance driver during the war, so he must have seen some terrible things after the bombing raids. People with their arms and legs blown off; bodies unrecognisable because they had been blown to smithereens; dead children and babies. No wonder he drank; there was no counselling in those days to help him deal with the horrors, just brown ale.

All that horror wasn't the reason he committed suicide, though. It was a year before the end of the war and the rumour was that my nan was having an affair, and someone who was out to make trouble sent Granddad a poison-pen letter telling him so. Not long after that, he took his own life. He was depressed, he'd had enough, and he put his head in the gas oven. A lot of people said it was a cry for help and that he had not really meant to kill himself, but he did.

Mum remembers the day he died as though it were yesterday. She was seven and Patrick would have been six at the time. They walked in from school, hand in hand as usual – they always held hands – and opened the door to find the house eerily quiet. Not only was it quiet, but also the smell of gas was so strong it was choking. She opened the door to their tiny kitchen, looking around for a welcoming, familiar face, only to see her father slumped on the floor, lying absolutely still next to the cooker and clutching the letter in his left hand. The oven door was open and the gas was turned on full. Mum knew enough to turn off the gas and open a window, then she touched him, but his hands were as cold as ice. She called his name, but he didn't answer. He was dead. Panicking, she froze, pulled Patrick to her and fell to the floor next to her dad, not knowing what to do. Occasionally she whispered, 'Dad, Dad,' and shook him but got no response. She has no idea how long she sat there, but she stayed where she was, rocking Patrick, in shock, until her grown-up sisters came home from work and gently lifted her off the floor.

After that, my nan, Hetty, suffered a nervous breakdown. You can only imagine the torment she must have suffered. No one ever knew whether she was having an affair, but in those days, as far as everyone else was concerned, there was no smoke without fire. My granddad knew that; he felt shamed and he took his own life.

Nan blamed herself for his death and the guilt would have been terrible, particularly as she was a Catholic. Suicide is a sin for Catholics. Their belief is that my granddad would have gone straight to Hell, and Nan would have felt responsible for his eternal damnation, no matter how often she went to church and confessed to the priest, and no matter how many times she said the rosary. And though the family tried hard, they never found out who sent that poison-pen letter.

So it's not surprising that Nan fell apart after Granddad's death. And from then on, she could not look after Mum and Patrick. They were the youngest of five, and there were ten years between them and their older siblings, but it still meant that my grandmother had five mouths to feed on her own, and even though the older ones helped, it was hard work.

The family decided it would be best if Mum and Patrick were evacuated, so they were sent away to live with foster carers in Wales until things calmed down. It was 1944, the war was still raging and there was always the threat of a direct hit from German bombs. Nan welcomed that for herself – she thought she deserved it – but she could not bear the thought that if her children stayed, God could punish her by taking them too.

Wales was a million miles away from London in those days and my mum and Patrick arrived at the railway station with their gas masks round their necks and brown luggage labels tied to their coats with their names and dates of birth written on them. They were bewildered and bereaved, and every comfort they had ever known was back among the bombsites of Catford.

If luck, or God, had been on their side, their temporary family would have been welcoming and kind. They dreamed they would be placed with a baker and his wife who served sticky buns for tea on a Sunday, but the couple they ended up with were cruel and uncaring. Their favourite punishment was to lock them in the garden shed for minor misde-meanours. Mum said it was dark, damp and full of spiders, with shadows everywhere, and she was terri-fied in there. Her main concern was protecting her younger brother, who was just as scared as she was. To pass the time, she made up stories for him, happy tales about ice cream and lollipops, of unexploded bombs and sunny days in Catford. She very quickly learned not to cry – they both did, because if they cried they would be made to stay in the shed until they stopped.

Both children were totally dazed. It was as if they, too, were being punished for their dad's death. That whole episode in Mum's life was a massive trauma, one she never forgot, and it ultimately shaped the person she became.

# Chapter Three

Mum and Dad had both had difficult childhoods, and they were also incredibly young to start a family; Dad was only seventeen when he married Mum, who was only sixteen herself. When my sister Rosa was born, Dad was eighteen, and only nineteen by the time I was born. He was the ripe old age of twenty-two when my brother Joe arrived, and twenty-three when Mum gave birth to Bianca.

Mum's two older sisters, Lily and Daisy, were very successful in their own fields: Daisy in fashion, and Lily, the stunning beauty of the family, was a secretary for a big furniture company. They had got out of poverty, married quite wealthy men and had good careers. Mum was the poor one in the family and her sisters kept her financially while my nan, Hetty, helped her look after us.

Nan thought Dad was not good enough for my mum, so she continually told her, in front of my dad: 'You are never going to have anything, because you've married a foreigner.' Dad struggled to fit in as it was. He got called 'English' in Italy and in London they called him 'Spaghetti' or 'Wop'. Wop was a derogatory term used for Italian immigrants. It was short for 'Without Papers', as many had come over without identity papers, and was common slang in the Sixties and Seventies. Not surprisingly, it upset Dad a lot.

It just brought home to Dad that he wasn't really Italian and he wasn't really English. Nan knew my dad never felt as though he fitted in and that the word 'foreigner' would really hurt him. It cut deep and she knew it. That's why she said it.

Dad could never do anything right and all Mum's family used to argue with him. If he spoke back, Nan would get up and roll up her sleeves. 'Get outside!' she would shout at him, and she would honestly have taken him on if he had gone with her. Instead, Dad would do the sensible thing and storm off until it all settled down. I dread to think what would have happened if they had come to blows.

Nan was a tiny grey-haired woman. She may have survived the war, but she was still deeply affected by her husband's suicide, although she would never show it or talk about it. Since his death she had done nothing but work hard and care for her family, and every bit of softness and compassion in her had been trampled on. There was no doubt she could be a cow. If Mum brought a friend home, Nan would say: 'Come on, clear off, she's got things to do.'

There was only one way that Hetty showed her love and that was through control. She had to be in charge and no one messed with her – they didn't dare. Hetty ruled the family with an iron rod and no one had better step out of line.

Although she could be terrifying at times, she was always there looking after us while Mum was at work, and I idolised her, simply because she was my nan and she was there for us.

My mum is a petite redhead with a lovely figure and a good sense of humour – if they had started making *EastEnders* in the 1950s, her family would have been mistaken for the cast.

You can imagine how volatile an Irish-Italian household could be, and Mum and Dad would often throw things at each other. They'd be having dinner and one of them would say something, and then, suddenly, there would be plates flying across the kitchen or saucepans being thrown at people's heads.

Mum threw as many saucepans as my dad, but neither of them ended up in hospital. Arguments and fights became so regular in our house, we thought it was normal. We thought everyone's parents fought all the time and threw things at each other.

It always seemed to me that my mum started the fights, but I suspect she was reacting out of frustration with my dad. Although they fought like heavy-weight champions, they never gave up on each other, which is so easy to do now. I like to think that they loved and needed one another and fought to keep the family together, rather than ripping it apart. I don't like to think that the fights had no purpose.

It is true that Dad was very violent and aggressive – not towards me, but towards my mum. As a child, I didn't really understand why Dad was so needy, but it was because Mum could never give him as much love as he needed. I actually don't think anyone could have, he was so damaged, so they would end up pushing each other around and me and Rosa would get in between them and try to calm them down, while Joe and Bianca sat on the sofa looking sad.

Like lots of other Italian immigrants, Dad worked at an Italian restaurant, but there was never any money. Dad was a gambler, so they had lots of money worries. He loved to bet on the horses, but he would also bet on football – anything, really – and his pockets were always full of little white gambling slips that he brought home from the bookies. He lost more often than not, but you knew when he had won, because he would come home with presents. If he had lost, he could go missing for days at a time.

Dad probably shrugged off a lot of responsibility, because my mum had her family network to support her, so why was he needed? When her family used to argue with him, I was always his ally and stuck up for him. He was never wrong in my eyes; he was never wrong until I was in my late thirties and I started to understand what kind of life my mum must have had with him.

I used to think Mum was mean and I hated her for shouting at Dad, but what I didn't think about when I was a child was how much responsibility she had. I never understood my mother; all I knew was that my dad made me feel like I was the most special child in the world, and whatever I did wrong, he stood by me. My mum, on the other hand, had three jobs and four kids by the time she was twenty-two and she had no time to mollycoddle me. Not only that, she had a husband who gambled away his wages. If only I had taken that on board while I was growing up, I might have been able to understand the stress and strain she was under and given her an easier time. Instead, I was always angry with her for shouting at my dad. What chance did Mum have with me? She would have got more response if she had tried to reason with the cooker.

Dad should have been the main breadwinner, but the responsibility for putting food on the table was down to Mum. She was exhausted half the time, because when she wasn't at home looking after us she was working shifts in the local pub or in the café, and when she wasn't doing that she cleaned the local school.

Somehow, their relationship survived, but Mum got no sympathy from Nan. It didn't matter how many plates got broken or how many saucepans got dented, how often she saw my mum sobbing her heart out or how often my dad went missing; Nan's response was always the same: 'You've made your bed, you lie on it.'

Was she right? I would say she was, because although it seemed harsh, she kept the family unit together.

We lived in Bermondsey at the time in a two-up, two-down. We had no boiler and no hot water upstairs, so we attached a hosepipe to the downstairs tap, threaded it out of the kitchen window and threw it up at the bathroom window until somebody caught it and we could fill the bath. The big problem was that by the time the bath was full, the water was lukewarm. The bathroom was freezing anyway, because you had to have the window open, so we sat and shivered as we washed ourselves clean. Even now, I can bath myself in two minutes flat.

I went to a Catholic school, obviously – being from an Irish-Italian background I would not have gone anywhere else – but I hated the nuns. I remember when I was about six, walking along the corridor to a class and because I started talking I was dragged out of the line. I had no idea I was doing anything wrong, but the next minute I remember getting the cane on my hand in the head teacher's office. Four times she hit me with full force. She didn't care that I was little; she held nothing back. The head teacher was a nun, and she was so terrifying I remember wetting myself, and then getting the cane again for wetting myself. I got no sympathy when I started crying; I was simply given a clean pair of knickers, told not to cry and sent back to class.

I know this sounds strange, but the nuns must have done something right because I loved school. We lived in a damp old Victorian house and one day, when my sisters, my brother and I were all in bed because we had really bad chest infections, Mum said: 'You're not going to school today, kids. Stay under your blankets, it's snowing outside.' Most kids love it when they get to stay home, but for some reason I didn't, so I got up, put my uniform on, walked out of the house without saying anything to anyone and went to school.

I went on to a Catholic secondary school. I left aged sixteen and my lovely Auntie Daisy got me a job at a magazine, working as a fashion assistant and earning £40 a week. I laughed when I saw the film *The Devil Wears Prada*, because my boss was just like that editor. She was incredibly elegant, with lots of blonde hair, big fur coats and high heels, and the whole office was scared of her. I was in awe of her because she was so inspirational and dynamic. People used to shake when she came into the room, but she just liked me. I don't know what it was – maybe all those years dealing with my difficult grandmothers made it easy for me to cope with 'big characters'.

I absolutely loved my job. It meant going to fashion shows and choosing models for fashion shoots that nine times out of ten were in exotic locations. It also meant I always had the latest clothes. I never wore anything more than twice. My local charity shop absolutely loved it when I walked through the door with my arms full of carrier bags. They knew everything in them was nearly new.

It was the Seventies, so I permed my long, dark hair, wore platform shoes and was given the first pair of designer jeans. No one had designer jeans in those days – they didn't really go mainstream until the Eighties – so I felt like a real trendsetter.

One night, when I was eighteen and out with mates in a pub in Chiswick, I met my partner Martin, a trainee black-cab driver. He had just turned twenty-one. I can honestly say it was not love at first sight, but I thought he had lovely blue eyes and he loved my dark Italian looks.

We fell in love and knew we were a perfect fit, but we never did get round to getting married – we kept meaning to, and then something would come up and we would put it off. I was working long hours, he was working long hours … Forty-odd years later, we are still wondering when we might have time to fit in a wedding.

We decided to move in together a couple of years after we met and bought our first house in Bermondsey. Martin's car was a gorgeous red MG and it was his pride and joy, but he happily sold it to get the deposit. The house was two-up, two-down and it cost £18,000. When we moved in it was totally derelict; everything needed doing, from the wiring to the plumbing. We weren't worried; we were young and unafraid of hard work, so every spare minute we had we spent on doing up that house.

Martin and my dad rewired, replastered and replaced all the plumbing while I did the fun bit, choosing the décor. Being the Seventies, everything was orange and brown, with floral curtains and wallpaper. A wicker chair hung from the ceiling and, of course, every room was fitted with a shag-pile carpet. When I talk about it now it sounds awful but then it was the height of fashion, and by the time we had finished I could not have been any happier if we had moved into Buckingham Palace.

We carried on with our busy lives, with me flying off every couple of months and Martin – who by now had completed 'the Knowledge' – driving his cab round the West End. We had no real routine, but we made sure we went out to eat at least once a week. We loved a good Italian restaurant, obviously, and afterwards we would go for long walks along the Embankment. We spent time getting to know each other, but we never lived in each other's pockets. It was not that intense love that can be so destructive, where you cannot be without each other for a minute. We loved being with each other, but we were both busy, we had our own friends and we are both close to our families, so there were not that many spare moments in the day. The love I felt for Martin was the kind of love that I knew was going to last. We trusted each other. I knew he was the man for me and he knew I was the woman for him.

Anyway, I was a career girl, one of the first, and I appreciated that my mother's generation had fought really hard to make sure that there were more options open to us than teacher, secretary or cleaner. We were the first generation of women who were really expected to go out and get full-time careers, and we did.

I worked hard and played hard, and children were not part of my plan. I had no desire to fall pregnant but Martin felt differently, and in the early days he gently tried to talk to me round, saying that he wanted to start a family. He soon gave up being subtle and resorted to nagging me whenever he saw a little baby tucked up in a pram, but I avoided the subject as much as I could. I loved my life as it was, being suited and booted and having a lot of responsibility. I had no intention of giving that up.

Despite our differences in wanting a family, our relationship was romantic and we were happy. We carried on like that for about four years. Then one morning, I woke up feeling sick as a dog. I thought I had food poisoning, as we'd been out for dinner the night before, but the next day was the same, and the next, and the next. I did not need Einstein to tell me I was pregnant.

There was no question I would keep the baby, even though having a child was not something I had really planned. Let's face it: if I had really, truly not wanted a child, I would have been a bit more careful, so let's just say my heart got the better of my head.

It was the middle of winter when Francesca was born, during the worst thunderstorm for twenty years. Then nine months later I got pregnant with my second daughter, Ruby. It was like having twins!

I had to give up work, of course. There was no such thing as a job share then, and my lifestyle meant that I would have needed a full-time nanny if I were to carry on. What would be the point? Anyway, I would not have wanted that.

I know people struggle financially when they have children, but my attitude is: change your lifestyle for a few years. I believe the first year of a child's life is really important. Children are children for such a short period, why would you leave them? And anyway, I was twenty-nine, I had been to every type of party you can imagine and I had enjoyed my career. I did not feel that I had to cling onto that; I felt I was moving into a new phase of my life. I wasn't going to put my kids in childcare; I wanted to do the caring myself.

Motherhood changes everyone's lives and mine was no exception, but if I am honest I missed the challenge of work. I loved being a mum, but I knew that I could take on more. Call it a sixth sense if you like, but I knew that a different path would present itself to me. I had no idea what, where or when, but I knew something would change. What I had no idea of then was just how much my life would change and how huge the challenge would be. What I took on next was a hundred times harder than organising a fashion shoot with a bunch of stroppy models used to getting anything they wanted. In fact, a few months down the line, I was often wishing I had it that easy.

# Chapter Four

I am a great believer that nothing happens by chance, and a shopping trip with my best friend Jane would change my life forever. I had known Jane most of my life, as I had grown up around her family and she had grown up around mine, and then, aged five, we started primary school together. I remember how our first day was full of excitement, anxiety and fear. We stood there wide-eyed in our straw boaters, our green-and-navy ties that we hadn't yet mastered the art of tying and our navy pinafores, which were a couple of sizes too big so that we didn't grow out of them too soon. We were little orphan Annies, and we looked at each other and smiled. I was not a pretty sight when I grinned, as I had no front teeth, which for some reason Jane found incredibly amusing.

Now she was getting married, but tragically her mother and father had both died. 'I'd love you to come and look for a wedding dress with me,' she said, and of course I wanted to be there for her. I could combine my two favourite pastimes: shopping for something special, and being with my best friend. So off we went with Francesca and Ruby in their double buggy. They must have been only one and two years old at the time.

Jane tried on loads of dresses, but nothing looked quite right. They were all either too flouncy, too plain, too low-cut or too high-cut, so by the end of the day she had no dress. I said: 'There's one thing we can do on the way home; we'll go to the shop in Bermondsey where my mum bought her wedding dress.' We arrived just before closing time, and she found the perfect one – ivory satin with a straight skirt, short train and tiny pearls embroidered round the neckline. We looked at each other across the room and both burst into tears. I was thinking how beautiful she looked, but I was so sad because her parents would not be there to see her on the happiest and the most important day of her life. She didn't need me to tell her what I was thinking; she just knew. That made us cry even harder. How we never ruined that dress with our salty tears I will never know.

We were both exhausted and starving hungry because we had been out all day. There was an Italian restaurant over the road and I knew the family who ran it. So we went in and grabbed a table. Sitting at the table next to us was a young woman with about seven children round her. She could not have been older than her late twenties, and her oldest child looked about ten and the youngest just a few months.

My brain was working overtime trying to do the maths, working out what age she must have been when she became a mother. Then, just as their pizzas arrived, one of the little ones decided she wanted to go to the toilet. The poor woman was really struggling, but because I talk to everybody and anybody I said, 'Don't worry, you go to the toilet and I'll watch the kids.'

When she came back, I asked, 'Are they all yours?'

'No, I foster,' she said.

I hadn't even heard of fostering and without knowing any more about it I said, 'I'd like to do that.'

This woman made it look so much fun, even though it was chaotic. There she was with all these kids, sitting in the restaurant having a laugh, with pizza falling on the floor and drinks going over, but it was obvious she loved it and obvious that she loved the kids and that they loved her. The anarchy of it all would have put most people off, but to me it just looked as though it was a happy table.

Going back to work was not something I was thinking about when this girl talked about fostering, but immediately I thought it was something that would fit in with my lifestyle. The opportunity came up and I grabbed it.

Before our meeting I had a very negative view of fostering – because of my mum and uncle's experience in Wales – but I could see that this was something totally different, so I told the woman I was interested. She said, 'There's a real shortage of foster carers in Bermondsey. Give me your number and I'll give it to a social worker.' I did, then went home and that was the end of it. I wasn't expecting anything to happen, but the next day the phone rang and it was Peter Inman from social services.

'I'm a social worker,' he said. 'I hear you're interested in fostering. Shall we meet?' After that short phone call, Peter would become a big part of my life for the next ten years.

I loved him; he was a down-to-earth northerner with a good sense of humour. He looked like a typical social worker – slightly geeky with his rucksack and desert boots – but you could have good banter with him.

When Martin came home that night I said, 'I've got a meeting with a social worker and I'm thinking about fostering.'

To which he replied, 'I'm not fostering. There's no way I'm going to foster. Forget about it.'

We didn't discuss it again, but I went ahead with plans to foster our first child anyway, because I knew once a baby arrived, Martin would come round. He did.

We lived in a borough where poverty was rife. Bermondsey was no different to any inner-city London district, with its wealthy and poor areas. In the wealthy part people lived in five-storey Georgian houses and drove Audis or Range Rovers. In the deprived part you regularly saw drug-dealers hanging around on street corners. It was comical, really. No one was supposed to know – the dealer and user did no more than bump their fists together – but you always knew money and drugs were changing hands. Then there were the alcoholics who sat on the park benches drinking cans of Special Brew for breakfast, lunch and dinner. They sat there, bleary-eyed, swearing and cursing at each other and occasionally starting a fight.

Like most other adults on the planet, these troubled people had children, and for some it helped them turn their lives around, but for others it pushed them further into their addictions – and their children ended up in care.

So it was against this backdrop that I started my training at the local foster carers' training centre. Sometimes Francesca and Ruby would come with me and enjoy themselves in the crèche provided by the borough, and at other times Mum would look after them. They were happy either way and I was enjoying a new challenge.

There were twelve of us on the course and I loved every minute of it. I sailed through most of the training on challenging behaviour, and quickly got to grips with bereavement, but there was one aspect that I found particularly difficult – sex abuse.

The most heart-breaking fact I discovered was that paedophiles tend to know the children they abuse. An abuser is commonly someone a child trusts, has grown up with and has shared family times with. They are the very people who should love and cherish a child in their family, and the very people whom a child loves and cherishes, but they are also the people who take advantage of that and end up destroying the children in their care.

The whole policy surrounding sex abuse troubled me. Once an abused child plucks up the courage to tell an adult what is happening, they are pretty much immediately taken away from the very people they love and placed with a foster carer until the child-protection work is completed. It is obvious that this is to keep the child safe, I understand that, but children often interpret that as a punishment for telling. I always thought there must be a better way round it, like removing the adult from the home or from the vicinity of the child, but it's never handled that way.

Once the abuse is out in the open, the child's behaviour can become extreme. It's likely that there have been warning signs. Typical ones are nightmares, moodiness, secrecy and clinginess, or a child may develop issues around eating – pretty much the same signs you would get if a child was suffering any trauma, such as divorce or problems with friends. Sex abuse, though, comes with an increased awareness of sex and sexual practices. You can imagine what a shock it is when a four-year-old starts talking about blow jobs or throwing four-letter words around as if they are talking about the Teletubbies. Advanced sexual behaviour in a child is always a worrying sign.

To an untrained adult, it can look as though the child is naughty. Bad behaviour, though, is often a cry for help, a cry they have no idea how to verbalise, so it comes out in misbehaviour. It is hard to take, though. For example, it is not unusual for a sexually abused child to smear their own faeces on the wall, develop problems with anger or to totally withdraw.

Sometimes I speak to adults who have been abused as children and who kept the abuse secret, never telling a soul until they reached adulthood, and I always wonder how no one noticed anything. How did no one spot that they were frightened, withdrawn and moody? Maybe people did, but it is a fact that most cases of sex abuse happen to children who are vulnerable in the first place, so perhaps there was just no one around to care.

They tell you how to deal with all this behaviour during training, but the reality is something else. Nothing can really prepare you for the task of trying to heal a child traumatised by sex abuse. At the time, I thought I was not ready to take that on and made a mental note to let Peter know.

During training you have lots of home visits, when social workers go into your background and find out if there are any mental-health problems within the family, whether anyone suffers from depression or if anyone takes drugs or drinks heavily. Family members who often visit your house all have to have police checks, and Martin and I both had to have a full medical. True, the assessment is quite intrusive, but it is similar to adopting a child, and with these vulnerable children no one is going to take any unnecessary risks.

A few days after I was passed as a suitable carer, social services rang to tell me they had a placement for me. She was a three-day-old baby girl called Sofia, they said, whose mother was an unmarried woman in her early twenties from Italy. What were the chances of that? Peter laughed and agreed it was incredible that my first baby would have almost the exact same story as my dad. It was like history repeating itself and I was being given the responsibility to turn what could be a terrible experience for this innocent child into a good one. All I can say is that fate has a really funny way of working its way into your life.

I immediately began having flashbacks as every moment of my father's story played itself out, frame by frame, like a film in my head. I felt his rejection and humiliation and how he had struggled to fit in, and I felt all that for Sofia too.

My father was a grown man, a grandfather and a husband, and Sofia was an innocent baby born fifty years later, yet they had the same story, the same start in life, and I hoped with all my heart that Sofia's life would take a different path to my dad's. I hoped that her guardian angel had other plans for her.

One thing I did realise immediately was that this was going to change my life in ways I could not foresee. That odd feeling I'd had all those months before, that some other path would open up for me, I now knew what it meant.

# Chapter Five

Sofia's mother had given birth in hospital and then disappeared without telling anyone where she was going. On the day Sofia was born, a hospital social worker called me. She was rather cold in her approach, giving me very little information about Sofia and basically just wanting the names and addresses of my GP and health visitor. She ended the conversation saying a social worker from my borough would be bringing Sofia to my house sometime in the next few days. I put the phone down and wondered if it was necessary for her to be that abrupt.

I waited and waited for Sofia to arrive – it was almost as if I was waiting to go into labour myself. I prepared Francesca and Ruby by talking about Sofia from morning till night. I told them we were going to get a new little baby, and asked if they would help me bath her and push her in the pram. They asked what colour eyes she had, why her mummy couldn't look after her and where her daddy was. I said that her mummy was unwell and I knew nothing about her daddy. Then they wanted to know how long she would be with us and whether she could sleep in their bedroom, and they each chose a dolly from their collection to give to her.

Social services provide all the equipment you need for a new baby and they had sent over a catalogue full of things we could order. We spent an afternoon going through the pages, choosing anything that was pink. We ordered a pram, a Moses basket, a cot, a bottle steriliser, pink babygrows, pink blankets and a pink coat. In fact, every item was pink.

It was exciting when the boxes arrived and we sat and opened them together.

We talked about what we would do with Sofia when she arrived, but I made sure the girls understood that she was not staying with us forever, and that although she was living with us and would be treated as part of the family I wanted them to know that she was not their sister. I added that I was looking after babies whose families had problems and were unable to look after them, but that they would hopefully go home in the future.

It was a Friday afternoon in mid December and I had just arrived home from the nursery with Francesca and Ruby when the doorbell went. All three of us raced to the front door, pushing each other out of the way to get there first. I won, of course. The social worker was standing there with a bundle and it was almost like the storks were delivering a baby, just like in *Dumbo*. Every Disney film has a fairy-tale ending and I was hoping that Sofia's life would be no different. I wanted the 'happily ever after' so badly for her I could almost touch it.

I had imagined an olive-skinned baby with dark hair, but Sofia had blonde hair and fair skin. It was a real shock, because her mum was from southern Italy, where everyone is very dark. No one seemed to know anything about her father, so Sofia could have inherited his looks. Whatever her parentage, she was a very pretty baby and I could not imagine how anyone could walk away from her. Baby modelling agencies would have snapped her up if they'd had the chance.

There are two social workers involved with every placement – one who acts for the foster family and one who represents the foster child – and they both arrived with her. Peter was ours and we had built up quite a relationship, so it was nice for me to see a familiar face. It made it a special occasion. Sofia's was a woman who was quite serious.

Although her mother had gone full term in her pregnancy, Sofia was tiny and she only weighed about 6lbs. She was so small that even newborn clothes seemed to swamp her. I knew very little about her, not because social services didn't want to tell me, but because they didn't know much either. What they could tell me was that Sofia's mum had checked herself into a local hospital, had delivered Sofia and left without telling anyone where she was going. Before she left, she had written Sofia's name on a piece of paper and pinned it to the blanket in her cot. That was the last thing she did for her, give her a name.

After that, social services got involved, but there were no records of Sofia's mother anywhere: no ante-natal classes, no doctors, no address. She just turned up, delivered her baby, slept, left the hospital and disappeared.

Information only came to light months later when an Italian couple in their fifties finally turned up at the social services offices to say that they were friends of the family, and that Sofia's mum's name was Maria.

They explained how Maria's family had contacted them from Italy and asked for their help. The couple were from the same village and had remained in touch with them for many years. They remembered Maria growing up and her family had asked them to look after her while she came over to England to have an abortion. They agreed to help, as Maria had got pregnant by a married man who had refused to acknowledge her.

Maria had flown over from Italy when she was seven months pregnant, believing she was only three or four months gone, so as it turned out it was too late for her to terminate the pregnancy. She then went missing about a month before she gave birth. When Maria didn't return to their house, the couple began visiting local hospitals until they finally found where she had had her baby, but by that time Sofia had been placed with me and the hospital directed them to social services.

I struggled with the contradictions of the Roman Catholic faith that dictates no sex before marriage because sex out of wedlock is deemed to be a mortal sin.

I could picture Maria and her parents, their faces wet with tears, clutching their rosary beads, sitting on a wooden bench, praying to the Almighty and listening to the priest repeat, 'In the name of the Father, the Son and the Holy Spirit ...' while calmly discussing how to deal with the problem.

Someone – either Maria or her parents – had decided that the baby should be aborted, but wasn't that a mortal sin? Was terminating the pregnancy better than living with the shame of being an unmarried mother and the shame that would bring on their family?

The most important thing Catholics are taught as children, and we are told it over and over and over again, is that you need to practise forgiveness. I wondered who would forgive Maria and who she could turn to in her hour of need? I wondered if she could forgive herself?

*Mia Marconi*

Fate decided that Maria would give birth to her daughter, but at only three days old, her history was already dramatic, but I felt secure in the knowledge that we could give her all the love and attention that she would never get from her own family – like my dad had never had from his.

We had a little welcoming party for everyone, with sandwiches and cake, and Sofia seemed to settle straight away. Francesca and Ruby just smiled and smiled, and when Martin came home he went over and gave Sofia a little kiss.

Sofia's social worker looked overwhelmed at the happiness we all showed and said she knew Sofia was going to be loved with us. She gave me lots of forms, and I went over them quickly as I wasn't really listening to anything she was saying – I just wanted a cuddle. She said she would visit in a few weeks, and that a health visitor would be in touch within a day.

Excitement filled the house. My entire family kept phoning and coming round to see her. It was truly like I had just given birth. Mum was the first to come round. She picked up Sofia and cuddled her, and then Dad arrived half an hour later. He was all over her, kissing her and talking to her in Italian, calling her '*Sofia bambina*'. He told her she had beautiful eyes. It made me feel really, really upset, because I was so aware of his family history, and yet he could still find compassion for this little child.

I never had much of a look-in with Sofia that first week as Francesca and Ruby took care of that. She was their own living dolly and they had no intention of putting her down.

They loved feeding her. I would sit them on the settee with a pillow under their arm so they could give her a bottle. They would sit and talk to her in her rocking chair and shake her rattle, and every time she cried they would stroke her hair or try to distract her. They were very sweet with her and I was overwhelmed with love for them.

Of course, they fought over who would push her in the pram and who would rock her in her chair. As the oldest, Francesca usually won, leaving Ruby crying, 'Mum, it's my turn!'

I was forever pulling them apart and it didn't matter how many times I said to them, 'You do it today, Francesca, and you do it tomorrow, Ruby,' they still fought over her. But that's the reality of family life. Anyone who believes it can be like *The Waltons* is not living in the real world.

Sofia slept in a Moses basket next to our bed. She was such a good baby. She rarely cried, except if she was hungry or wet, and physically, although she was small, she was fine. She only had one problem and that was with her eye.

When she was eleven days old I noticed that one eye was a bit sticky. I took her to see the doctor, who said it was conjunctivitis, gave me some eye ointment and told me I had to bathe her eyes every day with warm water. Sofia's health visitor said the same thing, and as conjunctivitis is very common in babies and I had already had two of my own, I knew this was the right diagnosis and was not that concerned.

It was a Friday when I took Sofia to see the doctor and on Sunday I went to visit my mum. Sofia's eye was getting worse and by the time I was ready to leave it was really swollen – if you touched her eyelid, big drops of pus came out. I was getting worried and Mum said that you couldn't mess around with eyes, so I took Sofia straight to A&E at Moorfields Eye Hospital. It is the best eye hospital in the world, so I knew we would be in good hands.

When we got there a doctor looked at her and asked me to sit in a room called STD, which I thought was short for 'Standard'. Well, I was a new carer and a bit naïve – it actually stood for 'Sexually Transmitted Diseases'. Inside the room they turned all the lights out and gently opened Sofia's eye, which was now firmly glued shut. When I saw what was underneath her eyelid I could not believe it. It was completely red, there was no sign of white anywhere and the lid was swollen with pus. I was so shocked I cried for her.

The doctor told me it was most likely the sexually transmitted disease chlamydia that was the cause, and that her mum must have had it when she was pregnant and passed it on to Sofia. I was dumbfounded. It would not have crossed my mind in a million years that that would be the diagnosis.

Sofia was prescribed special drops and I was told to bathe her eye every three hours. The doctor took a swab sample from her eye and said she was very worried about her, but told me to go home. She added that she would bike the sample over to the lab and ring me if the diagnosis was anything different.

I had only been home for about half an hour when the phone rang. It was the doctor and she said I needed to come back to the hospital urgently because she had some bad news.

I phoned a neighbour, who agreed to look after Francesca and Ruby. Then I phoned Martin and asked if he could get home ASAP, and once the girls were settled I went straight there. They were waiting for me and rushed Sofia into a room. They told me that the results had come back and showed that Sofia had contracted gonorrhoea, which could cause terrible damage if left untreated.

The doctor ordered special topical medicine from another hospital and had to have it biked over. Sofia was immediately admitted to intensive care and put on a drip.

A young consultant came to see me at her bedside. His tone was sharp and the way he looked at me – or rather avoided looking at me – made me want to fall through a hole in the floor. There was utter contempt written all over his face. 'You will have to stay for twenty-four hours, swab her eyes every fifteen minutes and put three different drops in her eyes,' he said, staring straight past me. He obviously thought I was her mother and had caused this terrible problem. I was fuming. I felt angry that Sofia was suffering and that he was judging me, assuming I was the cause.

Sofia had contracted this disease from her mother, who had gonorrhoea in pregnancy and had passed it on to Sofia during delivery. If Maria had told the doctors about it they could have carried out a Caesarian and it would not have affected Sofia, but she might not have known that she had it. I found out later that the symptoms can be quite mild. I was not going to judge her; after all, she could have been raped, and the doctor should have known that, whether he thought I was Sofia's mother or not.

I stayed calm and professional and told him that I was Sofia's foster carer and that unfortunately I couldn't sleep over as I had two young children at home. Suddenly he was very apologetic.

I went home that night and spent hours on the phone organising childcare for Francesca and Ruby, because I knew I would have to rush backwards and forwards to the hospital over the next few days.

The doctors told me when I returned the next day that they were really worried about Sofia. They said if I had not acted as fast as I had and taken her straight to A&E, she would have gone blind and eventually been brain-damaged. The disease eats through the back of the eye and into the brain, and the damage it causes is irreversible. The only thing that can stop it is antibiotics.

I was terrified. It was the early Eighties and in those days I had no idea about STDs and the effects they can have on a baby, but thank God I took her to the hospital, thank God for my mothering instincts and thank God for my mum reinforcing them. To think of the damage that could have been done if I had not been vigilant made me shudder. It was a good first lesson in caring and a really big shock.

As though I was her real mum, I visited Sofia every day and later took the girls too, who made her beautiful 'Get Well' cards. She was quite teary in hospital, and even after I took her home a week later she seemed really insecure. I was constantly worried about her and it took about a month before she felt safe again. As a family we were all overprotective of her for quite a while.

She still had to have special topical medicine and drops, which were so rare they still had to be ordered in advance and biked over. The day she was discharged, I left hospital with a massive plastic bag filled with sterile swabs, water, drops and medicine, and I had to continue her treatment at home for the next three months.

Every week we went back to Moorfields to have her eyes checked, and then to the Royal London

Hospital's Ophthalmic Department to have special drops administered, which really upset Sofia as they stung. Sometimes I was there for hours. Poor Sofia also got diarrhoea because of all the medicine, but despite that, and the fact that she was not even a month old, she was still a very happy baby.

I often thought about Sofia's mum at this time. She was still missing – she had not returned to Italy or contacted her family there. I thought about how difficult life must be for her. She spoke no English, had no family over here and could have felt very ill at times with gonorrhoea. I wondered if she had been treated and whether she knew that if she hadn't been, she ran the risk of becoming infertile. Sofia could end up being her only child.

It wasn't until much later that there were suggestions that she was a prostitute. When I told the Italian couple about Sofia's eye they started crying. The woman assumed that Maria must have been a prostitute, and the fact that she had no idea when her baby was due could have meant that she had been sleeping with more than one man. We really didn't know, though.

Although her family had no idea where Maria was, she kept in phone contact with the couple – but I never met her. I never knew what she looked like or saw a photo of her, and I often wondered if Sofia looked like her. More than once I asked them if they had a photo of Maria, but they always replied no.

Later on, they told me that there was a resemblance, although they said that Maria had dark hair, so I can only assume that it was her father who was blond. Was he English or Italian? Was he rich or poor, young or old? We would never know.

Six months later, Sofia was given the all-clear and no damage had been caused to her eyes. I was proud of myself and felt grateful every day that I had taken her to the hospital when I did.

She stayed with us for just over a year and fitted our family like a glove. She grew into a beautiful little girl, with blonde hair and the biggest brown eyes you have ever seen – every time I hear the song 'Brown Eyed Girl' by Van Morrison it brings tears to my eyes. The girls and I loved her to bits and we honestly fought over her like she was a dolly.

I would bathe her, put her in a pink babygrow, wrap her in her pink blanket and sit and gaze at her, wondering what kind of life she was going to have. Time flies when you hold a baby – one minute I would be doing her 10 p.m. feed and the next it would be midnight. One thing I noticed about her was that she never guzzled down her milk; she always drank it slowly. She already had impeccable manners!

Sofia was a bright little girl. She never seemed to take her eyes off me, following my every move, listening intently as I chatted to her in Italian, absorbing every little noise and taking in everything around her. She was also totally attached to the family and loved it when my brother and sisters, mum, dad, cousins, aunts and uncles popped in. She seemed really happy in the hustle and bustle of my huge family.

As she grew, she was never quite as confident as Francesca and Ruby and was sometimes quite nervous, especially when we were outside. Her big brown eyes would look around for reassurance, but she never had to wait too long before one of us came rushing to her aid, and it would usually be Francesca or Ruby who got there first. Her first words were 'Chesa' and 'Ubi', and her face broke into smiles whenever she saw them.

Bathtimes were a joy. She loved the water and her little legs would start kicking as soon as you turned the taps on. I often bathed all three girls together, and they would laugh and splash for hours. Sofia would sit inside a rubber ring that was secured to the bottom of the bath so she could not slide under, and they would play with all the bath toys. She also loved *Winnie the Pooh* videos, although really she had no choice, as the girls had them on all the time. And it was lovely watching her reach her various milestones: first crawling, then babbling and then, by the time she was one, she was cruising round the furniture.

Throughout the year, we had more contact with the Italian couple her mother had stayed with, but they still only visited Sofia half a dozen times. When they first came by they were a bit awkward and embarrassed with her – it was almost as though they were worried I was judging them. The husband was a jolly, warm man, the opposite of the wife, who had built an invisible wall around her to shield her from goodness knows what.

As time went on and she realised I had Italian heritage, she softened and became more open. She told me she was angry with Maria and blamed her for her family's heartache. Maria's mother was her best friend, they had known each other since childhood, so her loyalties were with her. She could muster no sympathy for Maria, only anger.

Whatever their personal feelings towards Maria, you could see that they cared about Sofia, especially the husband, who was far more tactile with her. He cradled her constantly, speaking softly to her in Italian, reassuring her that he would look after her. I had a feeling deep down that they would love her and care for her as though she was their own, but as I secretly wanted a fairy-tale ending for Sofia, I hoped that one day her mum would come back to get her. The fairy tale remained a fantasy and a decision was made about Sofia's future: the couple decided they wanted to adopt her.

Social services began sorting out the legalities with Sofia's grandparents in Italy, who had made it clear from the start that they did not want her. I suppose if they had taken her in there would have been too many questions for them to address. Southern Italy is far stricter than northern Italy, and they were from a small village, so there was no way they could have kept it quiet.

It's all too easy to feel angry towards a family who have rejected one of their own, but it might have been the best thing for Sofia. Social services do a brilliant job of trying to identify *any* family member capable of caring for a baby and they do not give up easily. I have no idea whether Maria's family was really dysfunctional or not, but whatever their story, none of them could take responsibility for raising Sofia, so the next best thing was for her to go to close family friends.

Sofia's grandparents did come over once to finalise the papers so that the family's friends could adopt her, but we never got to meet. It was a painful time for me, although I was prepared from the very start to lose her, and I kept that fact fresh in my mind on a daily basis. I knew the day she left I would feel heartbroken, but I knew I was prepared for it.

What I was not prepared for was seeing my two little girls' faces as I explained to them that Sofia had a new forever mummy. They were really crying and holding onto me, kissing Sofia, and I realised that no matter how much I had prepared them – and I had been telling them throughout the year that social services were looking for a new mummy for Sofia –

the reality was that they were going to miss this little girl who they had treated like their baby sister for a whole year – and a year is a long, long time to a child.

I had not expected this and began to wonder what the hell I was doing. I watched them grieve and they asked me over and over again: 'Mummy, why can't you be Sofia's forever mummy?'

Even more heartbreaking was when Ruby said, 'Are they going to take me away from you? Are you our forever mummy?' That really got to me and I cried, cuddled her and said that no, no one was ever going to take her away from me and that she was mine for ever and ever and ever, and that when Sofia went to live with her new mummy, she would be her mummy for ever and ever and ever. I told her that Mummy was there to look after other children until they could go back to their own families or find forever families, and again that she would always stay with me.

I dealt with it, but I began to ask myself whether by helping someone else's child I was damaging mine. I look back and wonder: did they need to go through that? And I still do not know the answer.

I confronted their grief head-on. I went to the library and got lots of books about mummies and daddies and families, and I did lots of drawings with them, showing all the different types of families you could have. I kept talking about Sofia so that they could tell me what they were feeling and I could deal with their hurt.

Sofia was adopted just before Christmas, which was just after her first birthday, and I wondered how it would be for her going from having two sisters and being in the heart of the hustle and bustle of our big, chaotic family to living with a middle-aged couple who had no other children.

I put that thought to one side as the kids and I made a memory box full of photos of Sofia with our family. There were pictures of the party we had had the day she arrived, there were pictures of her first Christmas and birthday. There were lots of photos of Francesca and Ruby playing with her, of her cuddling my mum and dad and Martin and me, of outings and other family occasions. I included her first dummy and her first outfit, and I also made sure that she knew that her eye had been infected and what it had been infected with. It is not a nice thing to know, but I believe there should be no secrets. My experience with Dad and Mum made me sure that it is best to know about your past and to deal with it. So many secrets had been kept from Dad, which damaged him a great deal, so I decided: *no more secrets*.

I handed the memory box to the social worker when she came to take Sofia. I don't know whether the box was ever given to Sofia, though, because once a child is adopted there is no guarantee that the information will be shared. The couple had the mentality that anything uncomfortable should be kept secret, so in my heart I have always suspected that Sofia was never told the truth and that, to this day, she knows nothing about me, Martin, Francesca and Ruby. It is hard to live with, but I have no choice.

After she left, we cried. We sat on the sofa and cuddled and sobbed together until we had no more tears left. Although I was upset, I felt I had accomplished something. This was nothing like all the other jobs I'd done; I had never had that same sense of achievement. I felt I had been in the right place at the right time, and I knew that I did not want to give up.

After she left, I never saw Sofia again. She would be nineteen now. I lost touch with the couple, but I did hear from a social worker who supported them for a while that the woman had suffered from cancer when Sofia was about three. I never actually found out whether she survived. It was sad, and I never stopped hoping that her mother had sorted herself out and come back for her. I cling to that fairy-tale ending for her, but I have no idea if she ever had it.

# Chapter Six

The nature of foster caring means that it was only a week or so before another baby came to us, and once that happened we began to put our grief behind us.

The new baby stayed for eight months, and Francesca and Ruby played with her with the same enthusiasm as they had with Sofia. They were still upset when she left, but it was not the same; their grief was not as fierce. It was right that they did get upset, because if they had stopped caring it would mean I had done something wrong, that they could not attach themselves any more or form close relationships. They came to an understanding about the leaving aspect of the process, that these children were part of our family while they were with us, but they were not staying forever. They knew who the 'forever' people in their lives were, and they knew that these babies were not in that group.

For the next few years I cared for lots more babies, whom I mainly collected from hospital when they were just a few days old. The majority of them had been born to heroin or crack addicts and were already on the 'at risk' register. Some of their mothers had already given birth to five or six (or in one case, seven) children, all of whom had been taken into care. There was little hope for some of these women – the sad truth is that only a tiny percentage ever kicks their habit and turns their lives around.

Their children are born addicted to crack cocaine or heroin and the minute they enter this world they are put on a special programme to help them withdraw from drugs. That is their start in life. My job was to pick them up, love and nurture them and do my best to help them until they could be placed with a loving forever family.

There is a lot of judgement of drug-addicted mothers, less so than of mothers who drink throughout their pregnancy. What is not generally known is that it is a medical fact that drink can do far more damage to unborn babies than drugs. It is a game of Russian roulette, really: some mothers can drink or take drugs throughout their pregnancy and be blessed with a healthy baby, while others will give birth to children with terrible disabilities and some might be so damaged they die. You can never tell what that bottle of vodka, crack pipe or syringe full of heroin will do.

\* \* \*

I will never forget Hope. Her mother was only fifteen and had drunk heavily and smoked drugs all the way through her pregnancy. Poor little Hope was born prematurely and there were complications during labour. She was very sick when she was born and was taken straight into intensive care. She spent her first few months in an incubator, but against all the odds she survived, although she was in and out of hospital during the first year of her life.

When I first saw her she looked like any healthy, chubby little girl, with her dimpled cheeks and blonde hair, but her looks were a mask. I quickly realised that steroids were responsible for her rounded appearance, and as I looked into her blue eyes I could tell that she was still very sick.

Hope was the quietest baby I have ever cared for; she was almost emotionless and very rarely cried. Numb because of the mountain of medication she was on, not only did she barely cry, she barely smiled either. There were rare times when her little face would break into a grin, and when that happened it was magical.

She was also the hardest baby to care for, and I had no idea what I was taking on. Although I had listened intently while the nurse explained how to care for Hope, there is a big difference between theory and practice. Any parent who has a disabled child will know what I'm talking about, but it is twenty times harder than anything you can imagine.

Hope lived in babygrows, as any other clothing would have been uncomfortable. She had so many tubes and lines stuck into her body that everything she wore had to be really loose and easy to get on and off. I will never forget filling a bottle-sized syringe full of formula milk and feeding it through a tube that went straight into her stomach.

I often thought I would like to buy her a dress, and I set that as a sort of benchmark. It seems silly, but it was really important to me. If I could buy her something frilly and girly, I would know she was getting better.

I never saw her as a disabled child; I just saw a baby who needed a lot of love and I was more than happy to give it to her. I always see the child before I see the disability. Any special need is irrelevant to me; I just want to love all children, no matter how damaged they are.

Most days I was confident that Hope would grow up to lead a fun-filled life, but then she would get one of her terrible, rattling chest infections and I would cry myself to sleep thinking that her existence would be full of pain.

I developed my daily routine caring for Hope, and with that routine came highs and lows, sleepless nights and constant prayers that mostly went un-answered. I remained positive and kept looking for the silver lining, and that was how I protected myself – by believing that there could be a happy ending for

Hope. Her name summed up everything I wished for this baby who was so obviously a fighter – hope.

When she came to live with us she was one year old and had spent most of her life in hospital. She had already had one foster carer, because Vicky, her mother, was not really able to look after her. Hope's carer, Martha, was a friend of mine, but she became so over-emotional about her that she fell out with Vicky. Vicky put in lots of complaints about Martha, but no one took any notice until a doctor witnessed her shouting at Vicky in front of Hope. She was screaming at her not to get involved and was telling her to go home. The doctor complained and Martha was struck off the foster carers' register.

I received a call from social services that came from the top. It was from a senior practitioner I had known for quite a while and got on really well with. She asked me if I would take over Hope's care and if I could do it quickly. It was awkward because Martha and I had recently had coffee together, and I knew she was very attached to Hope.

I also knew that it does not matter how negatively you feel about a child's parent; the one thing you cannot do is judge them. Martha had judged Vicky and had concluded that she should be kept away from Hope, and that was not a decision she was at liberty to make.

I could understand how she felt, but I did not agree with her. I always make every effort to treat all parents the same, because it really helps a child to know that you are friendly with their parents. The only time I struggle is when a child has been sexually abused. I find it extremely hard to look those parents in the face, and I do anything I can to avoid contact with them.

I spent many hours thinking about how Hope's placement with Martha could be kept going and I suggested various things to social services, but they assured me that they had tried everything. I knew that decisions like that were not made lightly and I knew there must have been lots of meetings where social services would have emphasised to Martha the importance of working in partnership. Martha must have known that this was the key to a successful placement, but for some reason she could not find her footing with Vicky. Maybe she'd just had enough of foster caring and was burning her bridges.

I knew that if I didn't agree to take Hope she would be placed with someone else anyway, so in the end I decided I should care for her and that, as a family, we were up to the challenge. I didn't spend hours and hours thinking about the decision, as time is a luxury to me. I tend to act on instinct, rather than intellectualise everything, so with very little thought I decided that we should go ahead.

Hope's disabilities were not frightening to me; they were not even an issue. Maybe I was naive, but what I thought was that I would love her, care for her and make it all right for her. Something I always fought to do for my dad – fix him and make it right.

The day she arrived we were all really excited. I was looking at the whole thing through rose-tinted glasses, even though she arrived at our house with mountains of equipment and medication.

My first task was to help her attach to a mother figure – me. She had spent so much time in hospital with no family member by her side that she had never bonded with a special adult, not even to one of the hospital nurses, because the ever-changing staff and agency workers meant that no one was around for long enough. There had been no familiar face in hospital to comfort Hope when she needed a cuddle, so she had missed out on bonding and had never learned to trust.

When babies bond with their main carers they develop confidence. They will always look around for the special adults they rely on when they start to get distressed. Babies communicate by crying and only those adults can interpret that cry quickly. The faster you know what a baby is asking for, the faster you can change their nappy, give them a bottle, take them for a walk, or whatever it is they need, and the sooner they stop crying. And there is nothing more joyful than having a happy baby around. When a baby smiles, everyone smiles.

Poor Hope could never be described as happy, and it was no wonder that she seemed distant and suspicious of bonding with any of us – there had been any number of people flitting in and out of her life, and none of them had stayed. I knew I wanted to put that right for her.

Francesca and Ruby were six and seven by now and both at school, which meant I had the whole day, uninterrupted, to care for Hope. A community nurse was allocated to us when Hope first arrived. I remember her so well – we bonded immediately. Mary was in her thirties, with blonde hair, small green eyes and a constant smile. She had a kind, homely face and her personality shone through. She always seemed to say the right thing at the right time.

She taught me how to feed Hope, what medication to give her and when, and she sat with me for hours answering my constant stream of questions, such as: 'How do I check the oxygen levels, and what is this or that medication for?'

Chest infections plagued Hope, so I had to learn how to massage her back and clear the mucus from her lungs, and then there was the mountain of medication, all of which had to be administered through her tubes. Massaging Hope was actually quite fun. Sometimes a physiotherapist came to the house to help, sometimes I did it alone or, if Vicky was visiting, I would ask her to join in and then we would have a chance to bond.

Walk into most babies' rooms and you will find musical mobiles, teddy bears and other toys. Hope's was no exception, although her room was also full of monitors and oxygen pumps, all there to keep her alive. Oxygen was piped through tubes into her nose at night from a cylinder that I had to change every other day. She needed it because she had been born prematurely and her lungs hadn't developed properly. If she had no oxygen she could stop breathing while she slept. The oxygen was measured by her sleep monitor, which was alarmed and buzzed if she failed to take a breath or if her oxygen was running low. Sometimes, if she rolled over while she slept and dislodged the tubes, the monitor would then buzz to warn me.

It could also buzz if there was a malfunction with the machine somewhere, and it was up to me to work out what was wrong. I needed to do that in seconds rather than minutes, because any delay could cause Hope to suffer brain damage.

It was like having a newborn baby, except magnified a hundred times. With a newborn you are so tuned in to their needs, they only have to sneeze and you wake up, so when the buzz of that monitor jolted me out of my sleep I leapt out of bed instantly and rushed in to see what was happening. A slow response could spell death to Hope.

I loved it in the morning when her oxygen tubes could come off. Once I had cleaned her face, I would feed and change her, then sit her in the highchair, where she would watch me while I rushed round dusting or preparing meals for the family. I will never forget how her blue eyes followed me everywhere, taking everything in.

It was just after Christmas when she came to live with us. As Christmas presents we had bought the girls puppies, two beautiful Jack Russell terriers called Jack and Jill, named after the nursery rhyme that we sang all the time. To say the house was hectic is an understatement, but it was full of energy, mischief and laughter, and I loved it.

As Vicky and I spent more time together, she slowly began to trust me and I gradually found out more and more about her background. She talked about her childhood and her struggles as a teenager, but the one thing she never said was who Hope's father was.

She did speak about her addiction, though, and said she had been in a bad place and was drinking and taking drugs to forget it all. It turned out that she had been in care for part of her life and had a fragmented relationship with her own mother. As a consequence, she suffered from low self-esteem and felt she was not worthy of love. Her first boyfriend took advantage of that and controlled her. He was the one who introduced her to drink when she was just thirteen and I wondered if he was Hope's father. It was obviously a painful subject so I didn't pry.

She had enough pain caring for her daughter, after all.

My feeling was: well, that was then and now is now. Let's move forward. Hope was here, and it was up to me and Vicky to keep her out of hospital and give her a happy life. We managed really well with her care and she never had to stay overnight in hospital during the nine months she was with me.

We did not talk about whether or not Vicky would ever be able to look after Hope full time. She had once had her own bedsit, but she had lost it because of rent arrears and now she was homeless and sleeping on a friend's sofa. She could not manage money at all and had no place she could call home, so the likelihood of her being able to care for Hope by herself was slim. I knew it was up to me to help Hope recover, and there was no doubt in my mind that I would be able to fix her. None whatsoever.

Vicky came to visit once a week and I never once smelled drink on her or saw any indication of drug abuse. I do remember her smelling of cigarettes, though, and she was continually asking to go into the garden so that she could have a fag.

I always thought she looked as though she needed a good hot meal. She was always nervous and extremely shy, and it was obvious to anyone who met her that she found it very hard to trust people. That was particularly evident when social workers were around. Vicky became withdrawn, sullen and distant as soon as one walked into the room.

We got on well generally, but at times our relationship was like teacher and pupil. Over the next few months we worked each other out, which took time, but eventually we built up a really good relationship. What was also lovely was the relationship Vicky developed with Martin. They were kind to each other and got on very well, you could tell.

I became quite protective of her and gradually our relationship changed from teacher and pupil to more like mother and daughter. I asked social workers if contact could increase under my supervision and they agreed. Vicky would visit three times a week and we spent those days caring for Hope together.

She was unsure of herself at first, so she never took the lead when it came to doing anything with her daughter. Her spirit had been crushed and she had no confidence, so it was hard for her to push herself forward. Despite her failings, she remained consistent, which is incredibly rare in mums whose children are in foster care. She turned up on time, she was sober and clean, she stayed for as long as she said she would and interacted with Hope while she was there.

The problem for Vicky was that she was needy and demotivated. She required constant guidance from me, and reassurance that she was getting it right. The reality was that because she still needed so much mothering herself, she found it hard to mother Hope.

For example, because she found taking the initiative hard, she would never think of sitting on the floor by herself to play with Hope, but she was quite happy if I initiated it. I'd sit with both of them, showing Vicky the gestures she needed to use to gain Hope's trust. Blowing bubbles, clapping hands and playing hide and seek are little games that come naturally to most mums – they are simple gestures a baby will respond to – but none of this came naturally to Vicky.

Martha had asked social services to stop Vicky's contact with Hope, saying that Hope became agitated when she was around. I never saw that happen, and in fact they developed a beautiful bond.

Hope began to thrive. It wasn't long before she started smiling at me when I went to lift her out of her cot, and not long after that she began stretching her arms up, wanting me to pick her up. Her body language had completely changed and I knew she was pleased to see me. It was so different from when she first arrived. When she saw me then she would look slightly confused, wondering who I was, whether she could trust me and whether I would be there tomorrow.

Now, she had begun to trust me and I allowed myself a small smile of satisfaction as I knew we were headed down the right road. It was when Francesca and Ruby came home that she really blossomed. The three of them would sit on the floor together, laughing and playing with the puppies, who had just as much fun as they did.

Every day with Hope was busy, as most of it was taken up by hospital appointments, visits from social workers, health visitors, community nurses, play therapists and physiotherapists. The list of tasks was endless and it all took up a lot of my time. At the end of some days I felt sapped of energy and barely had the strength to make a cup of tea. After caring for Hope for a few weeks, I began to feel a new respect for parents and carers who looked after disabled children.

I saw many doctors with Hope, but most of them seemed distant, cold and superior. Sometimes we would wait for hours to spend five minutes with one, only to come away feeling as though we had not achieved anything. I felt they were just ticking boxes. I understood that they worked long hours and saw numerous patients, some of whom could be pretty difficult, but it seemed like the caring side of the profession had disappeared. Few of them had time to sit and talk to us, few of them connected with Hope, they simply did not have the time – and we were made to feel that we should be grateful for the five minutes we were allocated.

While the days were always full for me, the nights could be lonely. We lived in a three-storey townhouse then. On the ground floor was a kitchen and a conservatory, the living room and one bedroom were on the first floor, and there were two bedrooms and two bathrooms on the top floor. Hope slept in the first-floor bedroom, so I sometimes slept on the settee in the living room next to her room in case she needed me, while Martin slept in our bed upstairs.

There were nights when I sat up with her, scared, because she had a cold or a chest infection. I was frightened she would wake up, need me and I wouldn't be there. There were nights when her alarm seemed to go off constantly, and some nights when I got very little sleep at all.

# Chapter Seven

For nine months Hope and I went backwards and forwards to hospital, I changed her oxygen cylinders and fed her through her tube. I massaged her back whenever her lungs were congested and we settled into a routine. The chance never came to visit mother-and-toddler groups because of all the hospital appointments, but when we could we spent time having fun in the park on the swings and enjoying family outings. The dress I wanted to buy for her remained a distant dream, but I felt sure that in a year's time the picture would be different. By her second Christmas, I thought, Hope would be celebrating wearing her first dress.

It was lovely to see her change. Emotionally, she was much happier, but her health stayed pretty much the same. She had good days and bad days, and there was still that daily mountain of medication she had to take. I was confident that one day she would turn a corner, but that corner was nowhere in sight. I could see that we had a long way to go before we would even see the curve of it.

Summer turned into autumn and the leaves on the trees were changing colour. My days with Hope were still pretty much the same, but on this particular day she seemed to sleep quite a lot. Extended sleeps were not unusual for Hope, as her illness – a combination of foetal alcohol syndrome, drugs, a premature birth and Vicky's poor diet while she was pregnant – meant that she would never be as fit and healthy as normal babies.

That night I fed her, bathed her, got her ready for bed and gave her all her medication, which I ticked off on a list. After her 11 p.m. feed, I settled her in her cot, attached her oxygen tubes, checked the level on the tanks, turned on her night light and her musical mobile and pretty soon she was drifting off to sleep.

I slept on the settee that night just in case, because I felt that Hope was not 100 per cent – but then again, she was never 100 per cent. I used to get a gut feeling just before she suffered a chest infection and I had that gut feeling now. Call it mother's instinct, but I just knew I should sleep on the settee.

It was 5 a.m. when the alarm went off and I jumped up and ran into her room. Hope was not crying or moving; she was lying in her cot and her lips were a blueish colour. I lifted her into my arms and screamed at Martin to help me. Hope was as limp as a rag doll and I held her tight. She was still breathing, but it was very shallow and she was unconscious. My whole body was quivering and I stood there screaming, shaking and calling, 'Hope! Hope!'

The minutes that followed were filled with despair. I was desperate for someone to do something – I didn't know what, so I was just running around the room screaming for someone to help me. I remember I looked up the stairs and saw Francesca and Ruby crying, 'Help Mummy, Daddy! Help Mummy!'

Martin looked at me as if to say, 'Don't scream, you're frightening the girls,' but I just could not stop.

He was the one who called the ambulance while I was still screaming. Incredibly, he kept calm and tried to help us all. He was our rock.

The ambulance arrived really quickly. They say that when you need one they take forever, but it seemed to arrive almost immediately. Martin was still on the phone to the emergency services when the doorbell rang.

The paramedics took Hope and seemed to bombard me with questions that I could not answer because I was still in a dreadful state. I managed to hand them the notes from the nurse and followed them to the ambulance. They put an oxygen mask on her and I could hear the siren as we raced towards the hospital. Everything seemed to be going at a hundred miles an hour, but when we arrived at A&E a few minutes later I breathed a sigh of relief – Hope was still alive; her breathing was shallow, but she was clinging on.

Doctors and nurses seemed to come from everywhere, and Hope seemed like such a tiny little bundle amid all the chaos. They took her away and I sat in a side room on my own, howling. I lost control of my body and sat there shaking, unable to talk. All I could do was wail. After a while a doctor came in to see me, and he had a nurse with him who looked lost. They said they were sorry, but they had been unable to save Hope. I just looked at them and screamed until my screams gradually turned into silent sobs. They had no idea how to console me and anyway I was inconsolable. After what seemed like a couple of minutes, they looked agitated and said they needed to move on to their next patient. They asked if there was anyone they could call. 'My mum,' I said, and they left the room.

Poor little Hope had died within minutes of arriving at hospital, having suffered total organ failure. Her heart, liver and kidneys had taken too much of a battering from the alcohol and recreational drugs, and the fact that she had been born before they were fully developed had not helped. Then the medication she was on to keep her alive had stopped working and her body had just shut down.

Mum came to pick me up and took me home. When she walked into the room I could see her face was full of sorrow and anxiety. She was sad for Hope and worried about me. I was grief-stricken and she almost had to carry me to the car. I remember hardly anything about the journey, but I know neither of us said anything. There were no words.

She was always brilliant when I needed her, probably because I was such an independent, determined child, constantly filling the house with injured animals that she had to help me care for. I remember how she helped me with my lists of things I had to do for them, and came with me when it was time to set them free. As if having four kids and my father was not enough, she had my lame ducks to deal with as well!

My dad never really coped well when I was at my weakest; he was so used to me looking out for him, he struggled when I was vulnerable and stayed in the background, but my mum knew exactly what to do.

I thought back to the meeting I had had with social services when we'd talked about the care Hope would need. No one had said that Hope might die, no one. Would I have cared for Hope had I known? My feeling now is that I would have cared for her anyway, because you never know what new medication or procedures will be available in the future. I would have stayed positive. My sights would have been set on that silver lining and the fairy-tale ending.

Hindsight can be a wonderful thing and if I really think about it, I knew that her chances of making a full recovery were slim. I was probably given all this information but did not want to accept or acknowledge it. I had convinced myself that it was going to be all right, because the alternative was just too hard to contemplate. Looking back now, I realise that no amount of love, no machine, no injection, no medicine and no miracle could have saved her.

I had agreed to care for Hope because I wanted her to have the best life she could, and the truth is that no one knows how life will pan out for a child with a disability. I knew that, but the one thing I was not prepared for was for her to die.

Hope's funeral was arranged within the week at a tiny local church where she would be cremated rather than buried. I was dreading it. I had never been to a child's funeral before and had no idea what to expect. No parent expects to bury a child; your whole life is dedicated to helping them grow up and mature, and although Hope was not mine I felt no differently about her. I expected her to get stronger month by month and year by year, to finish school, get a job, fall in love and have her own children, and I would have had the satisfaction of knowing that I had played a big part in making that possible. I had never seen this coming, and I had no idea whether or not I would be able to keep myself together, or even if it was right that I tried.

The saddest thing about that day was the handful of mourners. There was no big family turnout for

Hope, only Martin and me, Vicky, Vicky's mum, an aunt and a couple of Vicky's friends. Three social workers and Hope's community nurse also came, which was lovely as they didn't have to, but it just reminded me of the struggle Hope had endured even to get this far. Vicky's new boyfriend was there and was just as much a bag of bones as she was. As I looked at him all I could feel was sadness. He was doing his very best, but he seemed like a lost soul himself, and although they were both eighteen, they looked as immature as two young school children.

Martin was a pillar of strength all the way through. He had also bonded with Vicky and often said he felt so sorry for her. He'd treated her like a daughter, and as she had no father figure in her life she'd really responded to him. I got a lot of pleasure from seeing Martin banter with Vicky. As far as I knew, he was the only one who could make her smile.

Martin is an amazing man and he was a massive support to me throughout that whole episode. I don't think I ever told him so at the time, so he didn't know how much it meant to me. Some partners would have waded in with 'I told you so,' but he never once said that I should not have cared for Hope. Not once. And I know that he never thought it privately either. Secretly, he was proud that I was prepared to take on such a huge challenge, even if it had not turned out the way we thought it would.

Martin always has the right words to say, or he will say nothing at all – not so much the strong silent type, but he is wise and keeps his counsel. It was at times like this that I realised how much I loved him, and I promised myself I would stop taking him for granted.

Vicky was a gibbering wreck all day, shaking and sobbing. Her boyfriend was literally holding her up. I wasn't much better. She and I were both in shock. Who wouldn't be? We were there to bury a baby that we had loved and cared for.

It was so important for us all to be together, supporting each other. Vicky and I cried a river, wiped each other's tears and comforted each other. We could feel each other's pain, although I could not measure my grief by her grief. She was Hope's mother, after all. The thought of how we were going to live without Hope was devastating, and I kept thinking how I would never get to see her dressed in the lovely frilly dress I had pictured. It sounds so silly when I say that now, but at the time it seemed like such a big thing. I felt I hadn't managed to help her heal enough so that she could wear that dress.

I knew in my heart that I would recover in time, but I felt Vicky would have a tougher journey than me. It was daunting to think how she was going to tackle it. I wondered if she would do what so many in her situation do and turn to a syringe or a bottle for comfort.

It was sunny that day and I took it as a sign that Hope was free of pain. As I stared at her tiny white coffin, on which I'd laid some pink roses, I thought about how she had graced this earth for such a short while.

Vicky never once blamed me and at times that thought got me through the day. It may sound surprising but we were close, and when she wasn't holding her boyfriend she cuddled me and said that she was relieved that Hope had died while she was with me and not in a hospital cot, being looked after by a stranger.

The service was over quite quickly and afterwards we went back to Vicky's mum's house. It was rough and ready, with few comforts, but when we arrived Vicky greeted us with a cup of tea. We sat down and talked about what the world without Hope would be like and how it would be a sadder place. Caring for Hope had taken up so much of our day – as with all babies it had been a twenty-four-hour job, but with Hope it was like having five babies. Martin chatted to Vicky's mum and he said she seemed like a nice woman, so I wondered to myself: what was going on under the surface in their family for it all to have ended so badly?

After an hour, we said goodbye. Martin and I got into the car and looked at each other. We had no words. He just squeezed my hand and I could feel tears burning my eyes.

I turned and waved to Vicky. She looked sad and lost standing there, and I wondered what was next for her in life. I wondered if her boyfriend would treat her well and whether she would ever have any more children, and if she did, whether her time with me would have helped her to learn that caring for a child could be really rewarding. I wondered whether, if she ever got pregnant again, she would manage to stay away from drink and drugs or whether the same fate would be awaiting her next child. I felt that she would be able to cope better, but I never did find out as I haven't seen or heard from her since.

I cannot deny that Hope's death was traumatic. It affected me deeply but, looking back, I can honestly say that I am glad I was part of her life. I learned a lot from that tiny sick little girl. I learned that I cannot fix everything.

# Chapter Eight

We decided not to take Francesca and Ruby to the funeral. Whether we were wrong or right to make that decision I still do not know. Our decision may seem odd. My mother and her brother were not allowed to go to their father's funeral, and it affected them deeply. Mum often speaks about it now and never really got over the fact. I always thought they should have been allowed to go, yet here I was, decades later, doing the same thing.

There was only one thing that influenced me: I did not want my girls to suffer more pain. No child should have to watch a baby being buried, and I simply wanted to protect them.

The girls became very subdued and sad after that, though, so I drew pictures with them and asked them to draw what heaven looked like. I remember Francesca's drawing was sunny, with a big park and lots of sweets in every corner, while Ruby's had lots of dogs running around with other children. We talked about Hope, and how she was running around happily with lots of new friends and dogs and had all the sweets she could eat.

Slowly, I got back into a routine of school runs, after-school clubs and the park, and the girls helped me heal as much as I helped them. While they were at school I spent my time sorting through Hope's things and talking to family and friends, attempting to make sense of it all and trying to find peace.

When I started fostering I had no idea that it would take me down such a sad path, but now it had I immediately decided that I would never look after a disabled baby again, or any babies, in fact. I was determined never to put my family through that again, and I suspected that I would give up fostering altogether.

I was full of admiration for the doctors and nurses – even the standoffish ones – who deal with death everyday. I had no idea how they did it and still kept their sanity. Maybe I just find death particularly hard. I know that I go to pieces whenever I have to talk about it, but I was determined not to face a premature death again.

Martin was fantastic and let me talk to him about Hope's death whenever I needed to, but I felt so raw immediately afterwards that I needed something else, something on a deeper level. So a couple of days after Hope had died I asked Mum if she would take me to church. The door was closed at my local Catholic church, so we went into the Church of

England one nearby. I sat in the front pew, crying and praying, and it was not long before the vicar came out and sat beside me. By this time I was hysterical, but he held my hand and assured me that Hope was at peace. He said she had been released from pain and assured me that I had done everything I could.

The next time I went I took the girls. The vicar was fantastic with them. He asked them what death meant to them, and they said, 'It's when you go to heaven.' He agreed and then explained that Hope had been a very sick little girl, and that heaven was a place where she could be free of tubes and oxygen, and she would be running around doing all the things that little girls should be able to do. They were very concerned about who was looking after her, and he told them not to worry that her mummy and me were not with her, because there would be so many other people who would be there caring for her.

While they processed their grief, my girls continued to withdraw and over the next few months they were still unusually quiet. Normally loud and confident, they stopped dancing and putting on shows when they got home from school. All they wanted was to come home and have quiet time, and I let them. So instead of shows, they drew a lot of pictures for Hope, mostly of heaven, and we talked a lot about her.

Hope's death affected Ruby more than Francesca, because she was the younger one, so she had tended to play more with Hope. She was the one who stayed quieter for longer.

The school noticed too and called to tell me they were concerned because they were both so subdued, so I went in to see their head teacher and reassured her that we were helping them through it.

Social services offered therapy for them, but I have such a big family network I didn't think it was necessary. I spoke to the girls, my mum spoke to them, so did Martin and my sisters, and we had the vicar. I felt they had enough support, and so we got through it together as a family.

With time, their confidence and personalities returned, but I was shocked to see how severely the loss had affected them at that young age. I knew they were grieving, and it was right that they were, but it made me take stock and realise that although I was helping other children I had to consider what effect it was having on my own kids. They had built a relationship with Hope, they had helped me care for her, and one morning they had woken up and she was dead. Also it had all happened not long after Sofia had left their lives. So when social services called, I let them know that, for a while at least, I wanted no more children to foster.

\* \* \*

It took months for me to clear out Hope's room. I had to get all the machines and all the other paraphernalia that she had and return it to the various agencies they belonged to and it took quite a while to sort it all out. I could only do it in short bursts – too long in Hope's room and I would get distressed and start having flashbacks and I would begin shaking, then the tears would return.

When I could, I avoided her room altogether, but whenever I did go in, I felt cold and sad.

In fact, the whole house was tainted and I knew we had to move. Martin and the girls felt the same. I never told anyone who wanted to buy it what had happened there. What was the point? Anyway, we had no shortage of prospective buyers because it was a nice place, and it wasn't long before the estate agent plastered 'SOLD' across the 'FOR SALE' sign in the front garden.

We found a lovely new four-bedroom house a few miles away. I began packing boxes and as I filled them with the girls' toys and clothes, a memory of Hope's death would hit me hard, like a gale-force wind ready to knock me off my feet. When that happened I would visualise Hope's smile and remember the first morning she held her arms up to me, asking me to lift her out of her cot, or the sound of her giggling when Jack and Jill licked her face, or when she was playing with Francesca and Ruby. Momentarily, I would feel better, until the whole cycle began again.

As a mother, I was riddled with guilt at what I had put my children and partner through. I made sense of it all by telling myself that we had made Hope's life a little bit happier for a while. We had given love to Hope unconditionally, like any family would, and I knew that she'd had a better life because we cared. We had made a difference to her. It was important to remember that, and it was something that could not be taken away from us.

Our home held so many memories but I realised that, while living there, I had learned one big lesson: that life is for living and you cannot measure your achievements in money or possessions. The greatest gift of all, I decided, is being able to give your time without expecting anything in return.

My family had given everything, and now my heart was broken and my zest for life was ebbing away. I had to admit that I was exhausted, mentally and physically. I needed a rest from the tears that I could not stop and the thoughts – particularly the 'what ifs?' – that would not leave me alone. As a family, we needed time to regroup.

When the day came to move, the removal men loaded up our belongings in their van. I took a last look at the empty rooms to check we had left nothing behind, turned around and locked the front door for the last time. I will never forget the moment I shut it, because it was such a relief. It was like a terrible weight had been lifted off my shoulders.

We all piled into our car and it was mayhem. Jack and Jill wouldn't sit in one place and were clambering all over the seats, while Francesca held our goldfish bowl on her lap and tried to stop the dogs drinking the water. It was disorganised – or organised chaos, as I like to describe it – but that was our little family, and I loved us.

I opened the front door to our new home, and the sounds of happy squeals and laughter and dogs barking echoed in the empty rooms. I began to smile and I knew that life would go on. We would not forget Hope – it did not mean that, she would always have a place in our hearts – but we had to carry on living, something she had fought so hard to do.

I had no thoughts of taking another foster child then – we all needed a break – but I had not ruled it out. For the next year, I decided, it would just be me, Martin, the girls, the dogs and the goldfish. Then, when I felt we had all recovered, I would think about whether fostering again was the right thing to do.

# Moving Memoirs

Stories of hope, courage and the power of love…

If you loved this book, then you will love our
Moving Memoirs eNewsletter

## Sign up to…

- Be the first to hear about new books

- Get sneak previews from your favourite authors

- Read exclusive interviews

- Be entered into our monthly prize draw to win one
  of our latest releases before it's even hit the shops!

## Sign up at

## www.moving-memoirs.com